the
Mindful Life
Journal

seven minutes a day for
a better, more meaningful life

Created by
Justin R. Adams

Published by
Better Life Journals
ANN ARBOR, MICHIGAN
betterlifejournals.com

ISBN-13: 978-1-948337-00-7

Cover illustration by Elina Li.

CONTENTS

Inspiring

Enlightening

Preparing

Journaling

Integrating

Connecting

Closing

IDEAS THAT INSPIRE

"Mindfulness is awareness that arises through paying attention, on purpose, in the present moment, non-judgmentally. It's about knowing what is on your mind."

Jon Kabat-Zinn
*Creator of Mindfulness-Based Stress Reduction
and author of* Wherever You Go, There You Are

"Suppose you read about a pill that you could take once a day to reduce anxiety and increase your contentment. Would you take it? Suppose further that the pill has a great variety of side effects, all of them good: increased self-esteem, empathy, and trust; it even improves memory. Suppose, finally, that the pill is all natural and costs nothing. Now would you take it? The pill exists. It is meditation."

Jonathan Haidt
American psychologist and author of The Happiness Hypothesis

*"Any sufficiently advanced technology
is indistinguishable from magic."*

Arthur C. Clarke
British science fiction writer and author of 2001: A Space Odyssey

AN INTRIGUING PERSPECTIVE

EVERY NONFICTION BOOK IS AN argument. Here's mine:

A GOOD WAY TO LIVE A BETTER, MORE MEANINGFUL LIFE IS TO APPLY THAT ALMOST MAGICAL TECHNOLOGY CALLED MINDFULNESS TO YOUR EMOTIONS, INTENTIONS, AND ENERGY.

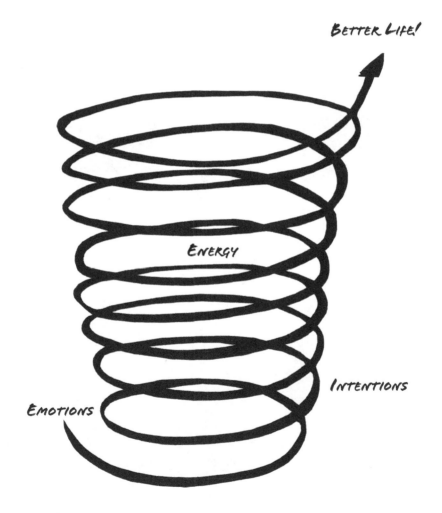

BETTER LIFE!

ENERGY

INTENTIONS

EMOTIONS

INTRODUCTION

WHY IS IT SO HARD to practice mindfulness in everyday life? You'd think it would be easy. After all, we take our ability to bring moment-to-moment awareness to our thoughts, feelings, and sensations with us wherever we go. Mindfulness is the most mobile technology of all; we're born with it. And, judging by the scientific research, it's practically magical.

In preparing this journal, I interrogated the scientific research, and the research makes mindfulness sound like a sufficiently advanced technology that is indistinguishable from magic. Here are some of the benefits according to the Greater Good Science Center at the University of California, Berkeley. Practicing mindfulness, even for just a few weeks, can help you become:

- Healthier by
  - » Reducing your stress
  - » Boosting your immune system
  - » Helping you sleep better
  - » Helping you fight off depression
  - » Reducing the risk you'll give birth prematurely
- Wealthier by
  - » Helping you create better relationships
  - » Making you a more confident, creative leader
  - » Making you more resilient to negative feedback
  - » Helping you and your partner feel closer
  - » Increasing your firm's customer satisfaction
- Wiser by
  - » Improving your memory
  - » Improving your decision-making abilities
  - » Boosting your self-compassion
  - » Securing your self-esteem
  - » Helping you act more in line with your values

Magical, right? Who wouldn't pay money for *that!*

For those of us who have done meditation retreats or studied mindfulness-based stress reduction, we know firsthand that the benefits of mindfulness are insanely great. Yet, it can be surprisingly hard to bring mindfulness into everyday life. According to meditation teacher and mindfulness guru Jack Kornfield, the most frequently asked question by students of meditation is: How do I bring this practice into my daily life?

Why is that?

Mindfulness Goes Against the Stream

I think it's because mindfulness goes against the stream. Like a raging river, modern life makes mindlessness the default option. It's easy to go along with advertising that promotes mindless consumption. It's harder to pause before buying to see if breathing is enough. It's easy to get sucked into the scandal and disaster that 24-hour news channels promote. It's harder to pay attention to the effects the media you consume has on you. It's easy to wolf down lunch without thinking. It's harder to eat with awareness and gratitude.

The challenge of living a mindful life goes deeper than simply consumer culture. The drive to be distracted is in our blood and in our brains.

In psychology, they say bad is stronger than good. Our biochemical systems are adapted to increase our chances of survival and reproduction. When someone cuts you off in traffic your body is on the job immediately. Faced with an imminent threat, anger can quickly become road rage.

Unfortunately, these biochemical systems don't care at all about whether we enjoy our experience. It can take conscious effort to calm ourselves and see the bright side of things. Getting control over our minds is so hard that in Zen, they call it the "monkey mind." Left to its own devices, the mind leaps from one low-hanging branch to the next.

To start living mindfully you have to stop allowing others or your biochemical systems decide what you attend to. As Austrian psychiatrist and Holocaust survivor Viktor Frankl said, "Between stimulus and response there is a space, and in that space lies our power and our freedom." To bring mindfulness into your daily life you have to struggle against the ceaseless currents of culture and chemistry. At first, it's hard to make any headway at all. Each time you stop swimming, you lose ground. It takes time to build your mindfulness muscles and to enhance your endurance.

A few years ago I attended my first 10-day meditation course. In the first three days, I learned how to tame the wild stallion that is my mind. Over the next seven days, I immersed myself in the sensations of my body. I discovered an inner world I had no idea existed. That experience altered the direction of my life.

While attending a meditation retreat is an excellent way to learn the skill of mindfulness, it's not the only way. And for most of us, using retreats to practice goes against the stream of life. Every time I disconnect from everything but my mind, my body, and the people silently sitting with me for ten days, I miss work or holidays. Or both.

When I set out to create *The Mindful Life Journal* I wanted to find a simple and effective way to practice mindfulness on an everyday basis. I wanted to get as many of those magical benefits as possible at the least cost of time, money, and effort.

This Journal Makes Swimming Against The Stream Easier

The Mindful Life Journal is designed to help you ease into mindfulness, one day at a time. It takes just a few minutes to fill out in the morning and a few more minutes at night. Over the next three months, the journal will be your daily companion, guiding you toward skillful awareness and deep insight.

With the help of more than forty volunteers, I've been testing the journal every day for months. Using the experience of these beta journalers as an indication; if you use this journal every day it will help you to:

- Emotions
  - » Feel better in the morning
  - » Discover what you're grateful for
  - » Listen to your heart more
- Intentions
  - » Be more intentional about your life
  - » Clarify your beliefs, values, and purpose
  - » Take actions that fortify and reflect your values
- Energy
  - » Increase your mood and energy
  - » Find the activities that give you the most energy
  - » Do something a little different each day

Now that you can see what you can expect to get out of keeping this journal, let's look at why it works.

Become Mindful of What Matters

Built at the intersection of ancient Eastern wisdom and modern Western science, *The Mindful Life Journal* helps you to become mindful of what matters: your emotions, intentions, and energy. With simple, practical prompts, the journal gently guides you towards creating healthy morning and evening habits. Each day you'll expand your emotional toolkit, align your intentions with your values, and use your energy as your compass. Over time, it will help you make mindfulness a habit and start living a better, more meaningful life.

Emotions — Expand Your Emotional Toolkit

From both a Buddhist philosophical and a modern psychological perspective, emotions matter. Two thousand six hundred years ago, the Buddha identified feelings as one of the foundations of mindfulness. The key, he said, is to know when you are feeling a pleasant feeling and when you are feeling a painful feeling, and to not get wrapped up in them. Watch the feeling arise. Watch it vanish. Take refuge in impermanence. No matter how good or bad it feels, the emotion isn't going to last.

Modern science builds on this ancient advice. It says that knowing something feels pleasant or unpleasant isn't enough. We need what psychologist Lisa Feldman Barrett calls emotional granularity. Having a fine-tuned sense of your feelings can help you experience more of life. The more emotions you can identify, the more tools you have to respond to the challenges you face.

Studies have shown that under intense distress, people who experience their emotions with more precision ("I'm melancholy" vs. "I feel bad") are less likely to binge drink, act out in aggression, or attempt to harm themselves. They're less reactive to rejection and experience less anxiety and depression.

On the positive side, emotions such as joy, gratitude, serenity, interest, hope, pride, amusement, inspiration, awe, and love help us to broaden our visual fields, think novel thoughts, engage in new activities, and connect with others. If negative emotions are the short game of life, positive emotions are the long game. Over time they enable us to accrue resources, become smarter, and stay resilient amidst constant change. To get granular with your emotions, you're going to take your emotional temperature when you wake up.

"I feel..."

Every day, the journal offers you eight different feeling words to choose from, while providing you space to write in your own feeling. There are 224 feeling words in all and they change every day. The emotions are here to help you put your feelings into words.

Neurobiological research shows that labeling the feeling of anger with the word anger turns down the response of the amygdala — that little almond-shaped brain organ that is hyper-vigilant for anything that threatens our short-term survival. Simply by labeling our emotions we can halt our inherent reactivity and shift ourselves into neutral. This is important because start-of-day mood inevitably affects performance. Feeling highly recovered in the morning increases your productivity as well as your likelihood of helping others during the day. Expanding your emotional toolkit will make you not just healthier, but wealthier and wiser as well.

You want to try to observe your emotions as they are, without resistance. If you feel sad, you feel sad. If you feel joyful, you feel joyful. Be present with the experience as it is. Don't react. Just observe. Allow the labeling to do its work.

From neutral, we want to try to adopt a positive orientation to the day.

"This morning, I am grateful for..."

Since bad is stronger than good, it's up to us to go "good hunting." We're going to do this by cultivating gratitude.

Gratitude is great. It's one of our quieter emotions. You feel it when you acknowledge another person as the source of your unexpected good fortune. When someone goes out of their way to help you, or when you are the beneficiary of an altruistic gift (think: clean, safe drinking water coming out of your tap in seemingly endless supply), you feel grateful. Feeling grateful inspires you to be kind and generous, which enhances your social bonds and increases your skills for showing care for others.

In experimental trials conducted with people aged 8 to 80, researchers have found that people keeping a gratitude journal experience 25% more joy, pleasure, and enthusiasm compared to people who journal about the hassles in their lives. Gratitude journalers feel 10-30% better about their health overall. They are less bothered by aches and pains, exercise more, have lower blood pressure, and higher levels of heart rate variability, which is a sign of a healthy heart. They're more sensitive to interpersonal relationships, more helpful, outgoing, altruistic, generous, and compassionate, as well as less lonely and isolated.

It's no wonder that 13th-century German theologian, philosopher, and mystic Meister Eckhart said, "If the only prayer you said in your whole life was, 'thank you,' that would suffice."

Now that you're feeling better, it's time to set your intentions for the day.

Intentions — Aim for What is Good for You *and* Others

The Tibetans say that everything rests on the tip of intention. They believe that what we get out of life depends on the intentions we put into life.

By applying mindfulness to our intentions we necessarily enter ethical territory. We have to ask ourselves often-hard questions about what is good and bad, what is healthy and unhealthy, what is wholesome and unwholesome. If everything rests on our intentions, we want to make sure we're pointing them in the right direction. We have to intend to become a good person.

But... what is a good person?

According to the Buddha, the finest kind of person is one who acts in ways that are good for themselves *and* good for others. He said:

> *Just as from a cow comes milk, from milk curd, from curd butter, from butter ghee, and from ghee comes cream-of-ghee, which is reckoned the foremost of all these, so the person practicing both for his own welfare and for the welfare of others is the foremost, the best, the preeminent, the supreme, and the finest [kind of person].*

The science of human motivation supports this perspective. There are two types of motivation that matter when it comes to intentions, one is called intrinsic motivation; the other prosocial motivation. In simple terms, intrinsic means good for you and prosocial means good for others.

We start with intrinsic motivation.

"I will make today enjoyable and interesting by..."

Would doing more of the things you find enjoyable and interesting make your life better? I think so.

The purpose of this prompt is to help you to design activities into your day that you'd happily do even if no one was paying you to do them. These are the kind of things you find inherently satisfying. You do them naturally and spontaneously when you feel free to follow your interests. They're fun for you. You often lose track of time while you're doing them. They're challenging but not too challenging.

Research shows that when intrinsically motivated, people feel drawn toward completing their work. They learn better, perform better, are more creative, and have overall improved well-being.

From practicing for our own welfare, we shift to practicing for the welfare of others.

"I will help others by..."

Would doing more things to help others make your life more meaningful? I think it would.

This prompt is here to help you to design activities into your day that will have a positive impact on other people. It's here to help you bring attention to things that benefit the families, organizations, and societies you belong to. It's here to help you contribute your unique gifts to something other than and larger than yourself.

If you're a nurse, that might be your patients. If you're a father, that might be your family. If you're a musician, that might be your audiences. If you're a banker, that might be your homebuyer. If you're a teacher, that might be your students. If you're a politician, that might be your country. If you're really ambitious, that might be all beings everywhere.

Research shows that cultivating prosocial intentions will help you take initiative, accept negative feedback, and keep going when things get tough. The pleasurable pursuit of your favorite prosocial activities will help you self-actualize, enhance your self-esteem, enable you to experience positive emotions, and increase your life satisfaction.

That's it for the morning routine. When you return to the journal in the evening, you're going to focus attention on your energy, because to achieve your highest intentions you need energy.

Energy — Use It as Your Compass

"Every great and commanding movement in the annals of the world is the triumph of enthusiasm," said American philosopher Ralph Waldo Emerson. He had a point.

Research shows that people who feel energized are curious, self-motivated, and full of life. Their enthusiasm is contagious. Their passion gets more people on board with their projects. They actively seek out the resources they need and produce more creative and higher quality outcomes. They're also mentally and physically healthier, feel more meaning, more self-worth, are more empowered, and experience more personal growth.

If that's the kind of life you desire to live, then spending a few minutes at the end of your day attending to your energy will help.

"Today, I was energized when..."

As you go about your day, take in everything. It can help to view your life as if through a wide-angle lens. That way when you sit down at the end of the day you can allow parts of your composition to emerge into your awareness. As you recollect your day, become mindful of what grabs your attention, without judging it. Bring an open, kindhearted curiosity to your energy.

When was energy present during the day? What kind of energy was it? What kinds of conditions repeatedly energize you? What kinds of conditions repeatedly took your energy away?

Look back at what you intended to do to make your day more interesting and enjoyable in the morning. Did those things actually bring you energy? Did your heart quicken? Did your eyes get wider and brighter? Were they fun? Did you get lost in the flow?

From observing positive energy, we shift to negative energy.

"My energy dropped when..."

There's a little death in every negative interaction. It takes time to recover from the things that leave you feeling drained, used up, tired, sluggish, and depleted. The strategy here is to become mindful of the people, situations, activities, or places that repeatedly take your energy away, and then exorcise those energy vampires from your life. If you can't eliminate the killjoys entirely, you can still become more resilient in the face of them. Again, don't react. Just observe.

Remember: Your energy is your compass. If you move in the direction of what lights you up, your enthusiasm will help you create the better, more meaningful life you seek.

From emotions to intentions to energy, we return to emotions in order to set ourselves up for the following day.

"This evening, I am grateful for..."

At the end the day, you want to remind yourself of the good things out in the world that make your life better. Even if that's as common as the free wi-fi at your local café. Cultivating gratitude at night will also help you sleep better. Research shows that people who keep gratitude journals actually sleep 10% longer and feel more refreshed when they wake up.

That's it for the evening routine. When you get to the end of each week you'll find a playful exercise to help you dive deeper.

Live a Better, More Meaningful Life

Keep on applying that almost magical technology called mindfulness to your emotions, intentions, and energy, and you're bound to be successful. If you do, I'm confident you will slowly start living a better life. Good luck!

Justin R. Adams
Ann Arbor, Michigan
November 2017

PAUSE TO REFLECT

As you prepare to start journaling, pause to think about the forces in your life that favor and oppose mindfulness.

Forces For Mindfulness   Forces Against Mindfulness

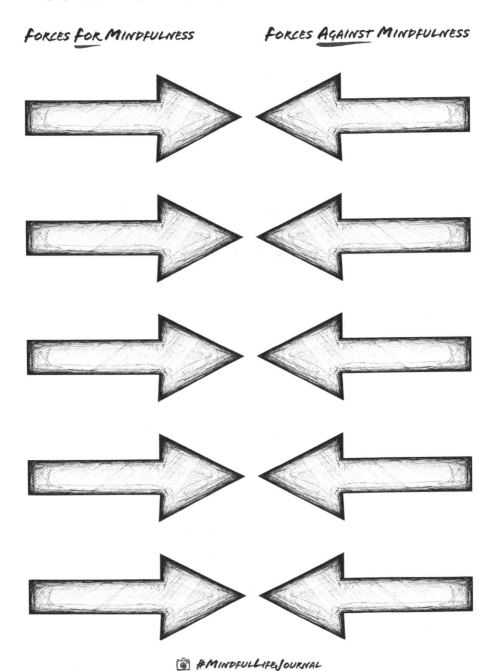

FOUR GOOD GUIDELINES

Whatever forces favor or oppose mindfulness in your life, the following four guidelines will help you get the most out of your *Mindful Life Journal*. Let's look at each.

1. Adopt a Mindful Mindset

"Our belief at the beginning of a doubtful undertaking," said famed psychologist William James, "is the one thing that ensures the successful outcome of the venture." That's why it's so important to pay attention to your mindset.

A Mindful Mindset is open, caring, and non-judgmental. It's a lot like a "beginner's mind" in Zen. It's about noticing what you have. It's about not wanting things to be different than the way they are. It's about working with things as you find them. What you're trying to do is to let go of control and be open to a wider and wider array of your experience.

2. Start Small

To successfully integrate mindfulness into your daily life, you have to make it a habit. The key to creating habits is to make the first steps of the new habit as easy as to do as possible.

When you start to journal, make your initial goal small. If all you do is identify your emotions in the morning, that's good enough. You've won the morning. Later, you can add in gratitude and intentions. In the evening, if you just write one thing that energized you, that's good enough. You can add the other stuff later.

It helps to do little things to remind yourself. For example, you might put the journal on your bedside table within arm's reach so that it's the first thing you see in the morning and the last thing you see before you sleep. Or you might place posters on your walls or stickers on your bathroom mirror to nudge yourself in a mindful direction. Get creative.

3. Share the Journey

We all need a support system. As the African proverb says, "If you want to go fast, go alone. If you want to go far, go together." Try filling out the journal with a loved one or a friend. Share what you're grateful for before you sleep. Use the *#MindfulLifeJournal* hashtag included on the weekly activities to connect with other

Mindful Lifers. Form a mindfulness-based journaling Meetup group in your local area or online.

4. Make a Commitment

Creating the life you want takes some effort. "The life that is worth living, and the only life that is worth living," said U.S. President Teddy Roosevelt, "is the life of effort, the life of effort to attain what is worth striving for."

By signing your name below you will commit yourself to keeping *The Mindful Life Journal* for seven days. At seven minutes a day, that's less than an hour of effort over the course of a week. You don't have to do all seven days in a row. The entry pages are undated. You just have to make a commitment to yourself to start.

Give the method a fair trial. See if it works for you. Sign now.

COMMITMENT TO CREATING A MINDFUL LIFE

I understand that I have the opportunity to create a better, more meaningful life for myself. I know that a good way to do that is to apply mindfulness to my emotions, intentions, and energy.

I freely commit to using *The Mindful Life Journal* for seven days. On each of those days I will spend seven minutes integrating mindfulness into my daily life.

I have read and fully agree to this *Commitment to Creating a Mindful Life*.

Signed: _____

Date: _____

CHEAT SHEET

A Quick Guide To Using Your Mindful Life Journal

1. Morning Routine — Narrate Your Day

Morning Emotions

- Select the emotions you feel this morning
- Write down any other emotion you feel

Morning Gratitude

- Write down two things you're grateful for (you'll feel better!)

Intrinsic Motivation

- Write down two ways you'll make today enjoyable and interesting

Prosocial Motivation

- Write down two ways you'll help others today

2. Evening Routine — Reflect On Your Day

Energizers

- Write down the people, interactions, situations, activities or experiences that gave you energy during the day

De-Energizers

- Write down the people, interactions, situations, activities or experiences that took energy away from you during the day

Evening Gratitude

- Write down two things you're grateful for (you'll sleep better!)

3. Each Week — Integrate Your Experience

The playful yet serious exercises at the end of each week are here to help you practice mindfulness, explore your emotions, clarify your intentions, and energize your life. Have fun with them. Use them to challenge yourself, integrate your experience, set your priorities, and manifest a more mindful life.

I feel...

| eager | edgy | grateful ✔ | hostile |
| pleased | regretful | wretched | zen ✔ |

a little tired

This morning, I am grateful for...

my best friend from college, for coming to visit me

the blue sky and clear white light this morning

I will make today enjoyable and interesting by...

getting into flow with my work

sending flirtatious texts to my special someone

I will help others by...

listening... seeking to understand before being understood

connecting the dots and offering my unique perspective

> Our belief at the beginning of a doubtful undertaking is the one
> thing that ensures the successful outcome of the venture.
>
> WILLIAM JAMES (1842–1910) AMERICAN PHILOSOPHER AND PSYCHOLOGIST

Today, I was energized when...   TIME **10 : 15 pm**

I finished my Brazilian Juijitsu class

that special someone responded to my texts

My energy dropped when...

I read the news today (oh boy)

I was doubting myself, thinking "this is impossible..."

This evening, I am grateful for...

all the coffee shops in Ann Arbor with free wi-fi

S.N. Goenka, for teaching me how to observe my thoughts

the
Mindful Life
Journal

M   T   W   T   F   S   S   DATE   /   /   TIME   :

I feel...   (absorbed)   (afraid)   (ecstatic)   (embarrassed)

_____   (happy)   (hurt)   (proud)   (remorseful)

This morning, I am grateful for...

_____

_____

I will make today enjoyable and interesting by...

_____

_____

I will help others by...

_____

_____

> **A mind which is not protected by mindfulness is as helpless as a blind man walking over uneven ground without a guide.**
>
> BUDDHA (C. 6TH CENTURY B.C.) INDIAN ASCETIC AND SAGE

Today, I was energized when...   TIME   :

_____

_____

My energy dropped when...

_____

_____

This evening, I am grateful for...

_____

_____

I feel...

affectionate	aggravated	elated	enraged
hopeful	impatient	quiet	removed

_____

This morning, I am grateful for...

_____

_____

I will make today enjoyable and interesting by...

_____

_____

I will help others by...

_____

_____

> Mindfulness is opening to or receiving the present moment,
> just as it is, without either clinging to it or rejecting it.
>
> SYLVIA BOORSTEIN (B. 1936) TEACHER OF BUDDHISM AND MINDFULNESS

Today, I was energized when...   TIME   :

_____

_____

My energy dropped when...

_____

_____

This evening, I am grateful for...

_____

_____

I feel...   (alert)   (alienated)   (elevated)   (envious)

_____   (huggy)   (insecure)   (radiant)   (repugnant)

This morning, I am grateful for...

_____

_____

I will make today enjoyable and interesting by...

_____

_____

I will help others by...

_____

_____

> We spend a great deal of time stumbling about
> distracted, veering from one thought to the next.
>
> STEPHEN BATCHELOR (B. 1953) BRITISH AUTHOR OF AFTER BUDDHISM

Today, I was energized when...   TIME   :

_____

_____

My energy dropped when...

_____

_____

This evening, I am grateful for...

_____

_____

M   T   W   T   F   S   S   DATE   /   /   TIME   :

I feel...   (amazed)   (ambivalent)   (empowered)   (exasperated)

_____   (immersed)   (isolated)   (rapturous)   (repulsed)

This morning, I am grateful for...

_____

_____

I will make today enjoyable and interesting by...

_____

_____

I will help others by...

_____

_____

You can't stop the waves, but you can learn how to surf.

JON KABAT-ZINN (B.1944) CREATOR OF MINDFULNESS-BASED STRESS REDUCTION

Today, I was energized when...   TIME   :

_____

_____

My energy dropped when...

_____

_____

This evening, I am grateful for...

_____

_____

M T W T F S S   DATE   /   /   TIME   :

I feel...

| amused | angry | enchanted | exhausted |
| inspired | jealous | reassured | resentful |

_____

This morning, I am grateful for...

_____

_____

I will make today enjoyable and interesting by...

_____

_____

I will help others by...

_____

_____

When we are mindful, deeply in touch with the present moment...we
begin to be filled with acceptance, joy, peace and love.

THICH NHAT HANH (B. 1926) VIETNAMESE BUDDHIST MONK AND PEACE ACTIVIST

Today, I was energized when...   TIME   :

_____

_____

My energy dropped when...

_____

_____

This evening, I am grateful for...

_____

_____

M T W T F S S   DATE   /   /   TIME   :

I feel...   (animated)   (annoyed)   (encouraged)   (fearful)

_____   (interested) (jittery)   (refreshed)   (reserved)

This morning, I am grateful for...

_____

_____

I will make today enjoyable and interesting by...

_____

_____

I will help others by...

_____

_____

**We must especially learn the art of directing
mindfulness into the closed areas of our life.**

JACK KORNFIELD (B. 1945) MEDITATION TEACHER, AUTHOR OF THE WISE HEART

Today, I was energized when...   TIME   :

_____

_____

My energy dropped when...

_____

_____

This evening, I am grateful for...

_____

_____

I feel...

| appreciative | apprehensive | energetic | fidgety |
| jovial | leery | rejuvenated | resigned |

_____

This morning, I am grateful for...

_____

_____

I will make today enjoyable and interesting by...

_____

_____

I will help others by...

_____

_____

if the ocean can calm itself, so can you.
we are both salt mixed with air.

NAYYIRAH WAHEED, INSTAGRAM POET AND AUTHOR OF SALT

Today, I was energized when...   TIME   :

_____

_____

My energy dropped when...

_____

_____

This evening, I am grateful for...

_____

_____

PRACTICE MINDFULNESS

CHEW A RAISIN 50 TIMES WITHOUT SWALLOWING.

WHAT DID YOU NOTICE? DESCRIBE YOUR EXPERIENCE.

M   T   W   T   F   S   S   DATE   /   /   TIME   :

I feel...   (ardent)   (argumentative)   (energized)   (flustered)

_____   (joyful)   (lethargic)   (relaxed)   (restless)

This morning, I am grateful for...

_____

_____

I will make today enjoyable and interesting by...

_____

_____

I will help others by...

_____

_____

**Our feelings are the source of our energy...
We should treat them with respect.**

M. SCOTT PECK (1936–2005) AUTHOR OF THE ROAD LESS TRAVELED

Today, I was energized when...   TIME   :

_____

_____

My energy dropped when...

_____

_____

This evening, I am grateful for...

_____

_____

M   T   W   T   F   S   S   DATE   /   /   TIME   :

I feel...   (aroused)   (ashamed)   (engaged)   (foreboding)

_____   (jubilant)   (listless)   (relieved)   (revolted)

This morning, I am grateful for...

_____

_____

I will make today enjoyable and interesting by...

_____

_____

I will help others by...

_____

_____

Emotion is the chief source of all becoming conscious. There can
be no transformation of darkness into light...without emotion.

CARL JUNG (1875–1961) SWISS PSYCHIATRIST AND PSYCHOANALYST

Today, I was energized when...   TIME   :

_____

_____

My energy dropped when...

_____

_____

This evening, I am grateful for...

_____

_____

I feel...   (astonished)   (avoidant)   (engrossed)   (forlorn)

_____   (intrigued)   (livid)   (rested)   (sad)

This morning, I am grateful for...

_____

_____

I will make today enjoyable and interesting by...

_____

_____

I will help others by...

_____

_____

**A man who is master of himself can end a
sorrow as easily as he can invent a pleasure.**

OSCAR WILDE (1854–1900) IRISH POET

Today, I was energized when...   TIME   :

_____

_____

My energy dropped when...

_____

_____

This evening, I am grateful for...

_____

_____

M   T   W   T   F   S   S   DATE   /   /   TIME   :

I feel...   (at ease)   (baffled)   (enthralled)   (fragile)
_____   (invigorated)   (loathing)   (safe)   (scared)

This morning, I am grateful for...

_____

_____

I will make today enjoyable and interesting by...

_____

_____

I will help others by...

_____

_____

All emotions are pure which gather you and lift you up.

RAINER MARIA RILKE (1875–1926) BOHEMIAN–AUSTRIAN POET

Today, I was energized when...   TIME   :

_____

_____

My energy dropped when...

_____

_____

This evening, I am grateful for...

_____

_____

37

I feel...   (awed)   (betrayed)   (enthusiastic)   (frazzled)

_____   (involved)   (lonely)   (satisfied)   (tearful)

This morning, I am grateful for...

_____

_____

I will make today enjoyable and interesting by...

_____

_____

I will help others by...

_____

_____

You cannot know what you cannot feel.

MARY WOLLSTONECRAFT SHELLEY (1759–1797) AUTHOR OF FRANKENSTEIN

Today, I was energized when...   TIME   :

_____

_____

My energy dropped when...

_____

_____

This evening, I am grateful for...

_____

_____

I feel... | blissful | | bored | | entranced | | frightened |

_____ | kind | | lost | | secure | | tense |

This morning, I am grateful for...

_____

_____

I will make today enjoyable and interesting by...

_____

_____

I will help others by...

_____

_____

You cannot make yourself feel something you do not feel, but you can make yourself do right in spite of your feelings.

PEARL S. BUCK (1892–1973) WINNER OF THE NOBEL PRIZE FOR LITERATURE

Today, I was energized when...   TIME   :

_____

_____

My energy dropped when...

_____

_____

This evening, I am grateful for...

_____

_____

M T W T F S S   DATE   /   /   TIME   :

I feel...   (bold)   (burned out)   (equanimous)   (frustrated)

_____   (lighthearted) (melancholy)   (self-assured)   (terrified)

This morning, I am grateful for...

_____

_____

I will make today enjoyable and interesting by...

_____

_____

I will help others by...

_____

_____

Never apologize for showing feeling.
When you do so you apologize for truth.

BENJAMIN DISRAELI (1804–1881) PRIME MINISTER OF THE UNITED KINGDOM

Today, I was energized when...   TIME   :

_____

_____

My energy dropped when...

_____

_____

This evening, I am grateful for...

_____

_____

EXPLORE YOUR EMOTIONS

Use this "index card" to describe and draw an emotion.

The Emotion:

It feels like:
1. _____
2. _____
3. _____
4. _____
5. _____

It Looks Like:

Consider creating (real) index cards for all your emotions.

M T W T F S S   DATE   /   /   TIME   :

I feel...

| calm | cautious | excited | furious |
| lively | miserable | serene | tired |

_____

This morning, I am grateful for...

_____

_____

I will make today enjoyable and interesting by...

_____

_____

I will help others by...

_____

_____

Everything rests on the tip of intention.

TIBETAN SAYING

Today, I was energized when...   TIME   :

_____

_____

My energy dropped when...

_____

_____

This evening, I am grateful for...

_____

_____

M T W T F S S   DATE   /   /   TIME   :

I feel...   (caring)   (concerned)   (exhilarated)   (gloomy)

_____   (lovey-dovey) (mistrustful) (spellbound) (torn)

This morning, I am grateful for...

_____

_____

I will make today enjoyable and interesting by...

_____

_____

I will help others by...

_____

_____

Intention is the seed we plant from
which effort grows and action blossoms.

ANGEL KYODO WILLIAMS (B. 1969) AFRICAN—AMERICAN ZEN PRIEST

Today, I was energized when...   TIME   :

_____

_____

My energy dropped when...

_____

_____

This evening, I am grateful for...

_____

_____

M   T   W   T   F   S   S   DATE   /   /   TIME   :

I feel...   (centered)   (confused)   (expansive)   (grieved)

_____   (loving)   (nervous)   (steady)   (troubled)

This morning, I am grateful for...

_____

_____

I will make today enjoyable and interesting by...

_____

_____

I will help others by...

_____

_____

Ultimately, the motivation underlying our pursuits should
not be wholly personal, but a desire to be of service.

VILAYAT KHAN (1916–2004) AUTHOR OF AWAKENING: A SUFI EXPERIENCE

Today, I was energized when...   TIME   :

_____

_____

My energy dropped when...

_____

_____

This evening, I am grateful for...

_____

_____

M T W T F S S   DATE   /   /   TIME   :

I feel...   (clear headed) (contemptuous) (expectant) (grumpy)
_____   (mellow)   (nostalgic)   (still)   (turbulent)

This morning, I am grateful for...

_____

_____

I will make today enjoyable and interesting by...

_____

_____

I will help others by...

_____

_____

Self-motivation...is at the heart of creativity,
responsibility, healthy behavior, and lasting change.

EDWARD DECI (B. 1942) CO-CREATOR OF SELF-DETERMINATION THEORY

Today, I was energized when...   TIME   :

_____

_____

My energy dropped when...

_____

_____

This evening, I am grateful for...

_____

_____

M   T   W   T   F   S   S   DATE   /   /   TIME   :

I feel...   (comfortable)   (cranky)   (exuberant)   (guarded)

_____   (motivated)   (numb)   (tender)   (uncomfortable)

This morning, I am grateful for...

_____

_____

I will make today enjoyable and interesting by...

_____

_____

I will help others by...

_____

_____

Each decision we make, each action
we take, is born of an intention.

SHARON SALZBERG (B. 1952) AMERICAN WRITER AND TEACHER OF BUDDHISM

Today, I was energized when...   TIME   :

_____

_____

My energy dropped when...

_____

_____

This evening, I am grateful for...

_____

_____

M T W T F S S   DATE   /   /   TIME   :

I feel...   (compassionate)   (dazed)   (fascinated)   (guilty)
_____ (moved)   (offended) (thankful)   (uneasy)

This morning, I am grateful for...

_____

_____

I will make today enjoyable and interesting by...

_____

_____

I will help others by...

_____

_____

You must live for your neighbors, if you would live for yourself.

SENECA (C. 4 B.C.–65 A.D.) ROMAN PHILOSOPHER AND STATESMAN

Today, I was energized when...   TIME   :

_____

_____

My energy dropped when...

_____

_____

This evening; I am grateful for...

_____

_____

M   T   W   T   F   S   S   DATE   /   /   TIME   :

I feel...   (confident)   (defensive)   (fearless)   (hateful)

_____   (open)   (outraged)   (thrilled)   (unhappy)

This morning, I am grateful for...

_____

_____

I will make today enjoyable and interesting by...

_____

_____

I will help others by...

_____

_____

**Tell me, what is it you plan to do
with your one wild and precious life?**

MARY OLIVER (B. 1935) WINNER OF THE PULITZER PRIZE FOR POETRY

Today, I was energized when...   TIME   :

_____

_____

My energy dropped when...

_____

_____

This evening, I am grateful for...

_____

_____

SET YOUR INTENTIONS

One way to remember who you are is to remember who your heroes are. Draw or paste pictures of your heroes here.

What do they have in common?

M   T   W   T   F   S   S   DATE   /   /   TIME   :

I feel...   (connected)   (detached)   (fired up)   (heartbroken)

_____   (open hearted) (overwhelmed) (tranquil)   (uninterested)

This morning, I am grateful for...

_____

_____

I will make today enjoyable and interesting by...

_____

_____

I will help others by...

_____

_____

You don't directly observe energy. You infer its existence through
its effects and you learn...to channel it to your advantage.

DEEPAK CHOPRA (B. 1947) AUTHOR OF JOURNEY INTO HEALING

Today, I was energized when...   TIME   :

_____

_____

My energy dropped when...

_____

_____

This evening, I am grateful for...

_____

_____

M T W T F S S   DATE   /   /   TIME   :

I feel...   (content)   (disappointed)   (friendly)   (heavy hearted)
_____   (optimistic) (panicked)   (trusting)   (upset)

This morning, I am grateful for...

_____

_____

I will make today enjoyable and interesting by...

_____

_____

I will help others by...

_____

_____

Passion is energy. Feel the power that
comes from focusing on what excites you.

OPRAH WINFREY (B. 1954) MEDIA ENTREPRENEUR, TALK SHOW HOST, ACTRESS

Today, I was energized when...   TIME   :

_____

_____

My energy dropped when...

_____

_____

This evening, I am grateful for...

_____

_____

M   T   W   T   F   S   S   DATE   /   /   TIME   :

I feel...   (courageous)   (disheartened)   (fulfilled)   (helpless)
_____   (overjoyed)   (perplexed)   (unafraid)   (vengeful)

This morning, I am grateful for...

_____

_____

I will make today enjoyable and interesting by...

_____

_____

I will help others by...

_____

_____

The influence of a vital person vitalizes.

JOSEPH CAMPBELL (1904–1987) AMERICAN MYTHOLOGIST, WRITER, AND TEACHER

Today, I was energized when...   TIME   :

_____

_____

My energy dropped when...

_____

_____

This evening, I am grateful for...

_____

_____

M T W T F S S   DATE   /   /   TIME   :

I feel...   (curious) (disillusioned) (giddy)   (hesitant)
_____   (passionate) (petrified) (vibrant) (vulnerable)

This morning, I am grateful for...

_____

_____

I will make today enjoyable and interesting by...

_____

_____

I will help others by...

_____

_____

Smile with face, smile with mind, and good energy
will come to you and clean away dirty energy.

ELIZABETH GILBERT (B. 1969) TED SPEAKER AND AUTHOR OF EAT PRAY LOVE

Today, I was energized when...   TIME   :

_____

_____

My energy dropped when...

_____

_____

This evening, I am grateful for...

_____

_____

I feel...   (dazzled)   (distraught)   (glad)   (hopeless)

_____   (peaceful)   (powerless)   (warm)   (wary)

This morning, I am grateful for...

_____

_____

I will make today enjoyable and interesting by...

_____

_____

I will help others by...

_____

_____

Like a healthy blood vessel, a high-quality connection
between two people allows the transfer of vital nutrients.

JANE DUTTON, AUTHOR OF AWAKENING COMPASSION AT WORK

Today, I was energized when...   TIME   :

_____

_____

My energy dropped when...

_____

_____

This evening, I am grateful for...

_____

_____

M   T   W   T   F   S   S   DATE   /   /   TIME   :

I feel...   (delighted)   (dreadful)   (good   )   (horrified)
_____   (pleasant)   (rattled)   (wonderful) (worried)

This morning, I am grateful for...

_____

_____

I will make today enjoyable and interesting by...

_____

_____

I will help others by...

_____

_____

**Living a connected life ultimately is about...
cultivating connection with family and close friends.**

BRENÉ BROWN (B. 1965) TED SPEAKER, AUTHOR OF BRAVING THE WILDERNESS

Today, I was energized when...   TIME   :

_____

_____

My energy dropped when...

_____

_____

This evening, I am grateful for...

_____

_____

M   T   W   T   F   S   S   DATE   /   /   TIME   :

I feel...

| eager | edgy | grateful | hostile |

_____

| pleased | regretful | wretched | zen |

This morning, I am grateful for...

_____

_____

I will make today enjoyable and interesting by...

_____

_____

I will help others by...

_____

_____

Inside of a ring or not, ain't nothing wrong
with going down. It's staying down that's wrong.

MUHAMMAD ALI (1942–2016) PROFESSIONAL BOXER AND SOCIAL ACTIVIST

Today, I was energized when...   TIME   :

_____

_____

My energy dropped when...

_____

_____

This evening, I am grateful for...

_____

_____

ENERGIZE YOUR PRACTICE

DRAW OR WRITE YOURSELF SOMETHING THAT WILL INSPIRE
YOU TO KEEP GOING WHEN YOU GET KNOCKED DOWN.

M   T   W   T   F   S   S   DATE   /   /   TIME   :

I feel...   (absorbed)   (afraid)   (ecstatic)   (embarrassed)

_____   (happy)   (hurt)   (proud)   (remorseful)

This morning, I am grateful for...

_____

_____

I will make today enjoyable and interesting by...

_____

_____

I will help others by...

_____

_____

The one serviceable, safe, certain, remunerative, attainable quality
in every study and every pursuit is the quality of attention.

CHARLES DICKENS (1812–1870) ENGLISH AUTHOR OF A CHRISTMAS CAROL

Today, I was energized when...   TIME   :

_____

_____

My energy dropped when...

_____

_____

This evening, I am grateful for...

_____

_____

M   T   W   T   F   S   S   DATE   /   /   TIME   :

I feel...   (affectionate)   (aggravated)   (elated)   (enraged)

_____   (hopeful)   (impatient)   (quiet)   (removed)

This morning, I am grateful for...

_____

_____

I will make today enjoyable and interesting by...

_____

_____

I will help others by...

_____

_____

**Attention is living; inattention is dying. The attentive
never stop; the inattentive are dead already.**

BUDDHA (C. 6TH CENTURY B.C.) INDIAN ASCETIC AND SAGE

Today, I was energized when...   TIME   :

_____

_____

My energy dropped when...

_____

_____

This evening, I am grateful for...

_____

_____

M   T   W   T   F   S   S   DATE   /   /   TIME   :

I feel...

| alert | alienated | elevated | envious |
| huggy | insecure | radiant | repugnant |

_____

This morning, I am grateful for...

_____

_____

I will make today enjoyable and interesting by...

_____

_____

I will help others by...

_____

_____

To pay attention, this is our endless and proper work.

MARY OLIVER (B. 1935) WINNER OF THE PULITZER PRIZE FOR POETRY

Today, I was energized when...   TIME   :

_____

_____

My energy dropped when...

_____

_____

This evening, I am grateful for...

_____

_____

M   T   W   T   F   S   S   DATE   /   /   TIME   :

I feel...
_____

(amazed)   (ambivalent)   (empowered)   (exasperated)
(immersed)   (isolated)   (rapturous)   (repulsed)

This morning, I am grateful for...

_____

_____

I will make today enjoyable and interesting by...

_____

_____

I will help others by...

_____

_____

> Nature has given us two ears, two eyes and but one tongue, to the
> end that we should hear and see more than we speak.
>
> **SOCRATES (469–399 B.C.) ANCIENT GREEK PHILOSOPHER**

Today, I was energized when...   TIME   :

_____

_____

My energy dropped when...

_____

_____

This evening, I am grateful for...

_____

_____

M   T   W   T   F   S   S   DATE   /   /   TIME   :

I feel...   (amused)   (angry)   (enchanted)   (exhausted)

_____   (inspired)   (jealous)   (reassured)   (resentful)

This morning, I am grateful for...

_____

_____

I will make today enjoyable and interesting by...

_____

_____

I will help others by...

_____

_____

A traveler without observation is a bird without wings.

MUSLIH SA'ADI (1184–1283) PERSIAN POET

Today, I was energized when...   TIME   :

_____

_____

My energy dropped when...

_____

_____

This evening, I am grateful for...

_____

_____

M   T   W   T   F   .S   S   DATE   /   /   TIME   :

I feel...   [animated]   [annoyed]   [encouraged]   [fearful]

_____   [interested]   [jittery]   [refreshed]   [reserved]

This morning, I am grateful for...

_____

_____

I will make today enjoyable and interesting by...

_____

_____

I will help others by...

_____

_____

Watchfulness...is the vital need, for he who does not watch is soon
overwhelmed. The sternman need only sleep a moment and the vessel is lost.

EPICTETUS (50–135) GREEK STOIC PHILOSOPHER

Today, I was energized when...   TIME   :

_____

_____

My energy dropped when...

_____

_____

This evening, I am grateful for...

_____

_____

M T W T F S S   DATE   /   /   TIME   :

I feel...
_____

(appreciative) (apprehensive) (energetic) (fidgety)
(jovial)   (leery)   (rejuvenated) (resigned)

This morning, I am grateful for...

_____

_____

I will make today enjoyable and interesting by...

_____

_____

I will help others by...

_____

_____

Real generosity toward the future lies in giving all to the present.

ALBERT CAMUS (1913–1960) FRENCH WRITER

Today, I was energized when...   TIME   :

_____

_____

My energy dropped when...

_____

_____

This evening, I am grateful for...

_____

_____

PRACTICE MINDFULNESS

WHAT ARE YOU SEEING, SMELLING, TASTING, TOUCHING, HEARING, AND THINKING IN THIS VERY MOMENT?

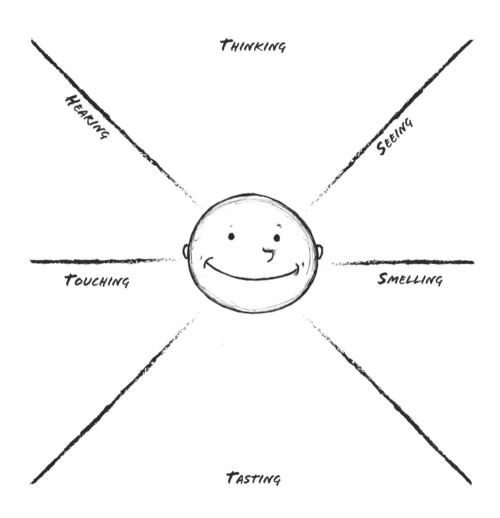

THINKING

HEARING

SEEING

TOUCHING

SMELLING

TASTING

M T W T F S S   DATE   /   /   TIME   :

I feel...   (ardent)   (argumentative)   (energized)   (flustered)

_____   (joyful)   (lethargic)   (relaxed)   (restless)

This morning, I am grateful for...

_____

_____

I will make today enjoyable and interesting by...

_____

_____

I will help others by...

_____

_____

**We often take for granted the very
things that most deserve our gratitude.**

CYNTHIA OZICK (B. 1928) AMERICAN NOVELIST AND ESSAYIST

Today, I was energized when...   TIME   :

_____

_____

My energy dropped when...

_____

_____

This evening, I am grateful for...

_____

_____

I feel...

(aroused) (ashamed) (engaged) (foreboding)

_____ (jubilant) (listless) (relieved) (revolted)

This morning, I am grateful for...

_____

_____

I will make today enjoyable and interesting by...

_____

_____

I will help others by...

_____

_____

> **If the only prayer you said in your whole
> life was, 'thank you,' that would suffice.**
>
> MEISTER ECKHART (1260–1328) GERMAN THEOLOGIAN AND MYSTIC

Today, I was energized when...   TIME   :

_____

_____

My energy dropped when...

_____

_____

This evening, I am grateful for...

_____

_____

I feel...   (astonished)   (avoidant)   (engrossed)   (forlorn)

_____   (intrigued)   (livid)   (rested)   (sad)

This morning, I am grateful for...

_____

_____

I will make today enjoyable and interesting by...

_____

_____

I will help others by...

_____

_____

When you arise in the morning, think of what a privilege it is to
be alive — to breathe, to think, to enjoy, to love.

MARCUS AURELIUS (121–180) STOIC PHILOSOPHER AND EMPEROR OF ROME

Today, I was energized when...   TIME   :

_____

_____

My energy dropped when...

_____

_____

This evening, I am grateful for...

_____

_____

M   T   W   T   F   S   S   DATE   /   /   TIME   :

I feel...

(at ease)   (baffled)   (enthralled)   (fragile)

_____   (invigorated)   (loathing)   (safe)   (scared)

This morning, I am grateful for...

_____

_____

I will make today enjoyable and interesting by...

_____

_____

I will help others by...

_____

_____

So much has been given to me; I have not time
to ponder over that which has been denied.

HELEN KELLER (1880–1968) 1ST DEAF–BLIND PERSON TO EARN A COLLEGE DEGREE

Today, I was energized when...   TIME   :

_____

_____

My energy dropped when...

_____

_____

This evening, I am grateful for...

_____

_____

M   T   W   T   F   S   S   DATE   /   /   TIME   :

I feel...   (awed)   (betrayed)   (enthusiastic)   (frazzled)

_____ (involved)   (lonely)   (satisfied)   (tearful)

This morning, I am grateful for...

_____

_____

I will make today enjoyable and interesting by...

_____

_____

I will help others by...

_____

_____

If you concentrate on finding whatever is good in every situation, you
will discover that your life will suddenly be filled with gratitude.

HAROLD KUSHNER (B. 1935) AUTHOR OF NINE ESSENTIAL THINGS I'VE LEARNED ABOUT LIFE

Today, I was energized when...   TIME   :

_____

_____

My energy dropped when...

_____

_____

This evening, I am grateful for...

_____

_____

M   T   W   T   F   S   S   DATE   /   /   TIME   :

I feel...   (blissful)   (bored)   (entranced)   (frightened)

_____   (kind)   (lost)   (secure)   (tense)

This morning, I am grateful for...

_____

_____

I will make today enjoyable and interesting by...

_____

_____

I will help others by...

_____

_____

It's also helpful to realize that this very body that we have...is
exactly what we need to be fully human, fully awake, fully alive.

PEMA CHODRON (B. 1936) AMERICAN-BORN TIBETAN BUDDHIST NUN

Today, I was energized when...   TIME   :

_____

_____

My energy dropped when...

_____

_____

This evening, I am grateful for...

_____

_____

M T W T F S S   DATE   /   /   TIME   :

I feel...   (bold)   (burned out)   (equanimous)   (frustrated)

_____   (lighthearted)   (melancholy)   (self-assured)   (terrified)

This morning, I am grateful for...

_____

_____

I will make today enjoyable and interesting by...

_____

_____

I will help others by...

_____

_____

Acknowledging the good that you already have in
your life is the foundation for all abundance.

ECKHART TOLLE (B. 1948) AUTHOR OF THE POWER OF NOW

Today, I was energized when...   TIME   :

_____

_____

My energy dropped when...

_____

_____

This evening, I am grateful for...

_____

_____

EXPLORE YOUR EMOTIONS

LOOKING BACK AT YOUR ENTRIES, WHAT ARE THE THREE THINGS YOU'RE MOST GRATEFUL FOR SO FAR?

 1.

 2.

 3.

M   T   W   T   F   S   S   DATE   /   /   TIME   :

I feel...

- (calm)
- (cautious)
- (excited)
- (furious)

_____

- (lively)
- (miserable)
- (serene)
- (tired)

This morning, I am grateful for...

_____

_____

I will make today enjoyable and interesting by...

_____

_____

I will help others by...

_____

_____

Where there's life, there's hope.

TERENCE (195–159 B.C.) ROMAN PLAYWRIGHT AND FREED SLAVE

Today, I was energized when...   TIME   :

_____

_____

My energy dropped when...

_____

_____

This evening, I am grateful for...

_____

_____

M   T   W   T   F   S   S   DATE   /   /   TIME   :

I feel...   (caring)   (concerned)   (exhilarated)   (gloomy)
_____   (lovey-dovey)   (mistrustful)   (spellbound)   (torn)

This morning, I am grateful for...

_____

_____

I will make today enjoyable and interesting by...

_____

_____

I will help others by...

_____

_____

Hope is being able to see that there
is light despite all of the darkness.

DESMOND TUTU (B. 1931) SOUTH AFRICAN NOBEL PEACE PRIZE WINNER

Today, I was energized when...   TIME   :

_____

_____

My energy dropped when...

_____

_____

This evening, I am grateful for...

_____

_____

I feel...   (centered)   (confused)   (expansive)   (grieved)

_____   (loving)   (nervous)   (steady)   (troubled)

This morning, I am grateful for...

_____

_____

I will make today enjoyable and interesting by...

_____

_____

I will help others by...

_____

_____

Three grand essentials to happiness in this life are something to do, something to love, and something to hope for.

JOSEPH ADDISON (1672–1719) ENGLISH ESSAYIST, POET, AND POLITICIAN

Today, I was energized when...   TIME   :

_____

_____

My energy dropped when...

_____

_____

This evening, I am grateful for...

_____

_____

M T W T F S S   DATE   /   /   TIME   :

I feel...   (clear headed) (contemptuous) (expectant) (grumpy)

_____   (mellow)   (nostalgic)   (still)   (turbulent)

This morning, I am grateful for...

_____

_____

I will make today enjoyable and interesting by...

_____

_____

I will help others by...

_____

_____

If we believe that tomorrow will be
better, we can bear a hardship today.

THICH NHAT HANH (B. 1926) VIETNAMESE BUDDHIST MONK AND PEACE ACTIVIST

Today, I was energized when...   TIME   :

_____

_____

My energy dropped when...

_____

_____

This evening, I am grateful for...

_____

_____

M   T   W   T   F   S   S   DATE   /   /   TIME   :

I feel...

(comfortable) (cranky) (exuberant) (guarded)
_____ (motivated) (numb) (tender) (uncomfortable)

This morning, I am grateful for...

_____

_____

I will make today enjoyable and interesting by...

_____

_____

I will help others by...

_____

_____

> We do not need magic to change the world, we carry all the power we
> need inside ourselves already: we have the power to imagine better.
>
> J.K. ROWLING (B. 1965) AUTHOR OF HARRY POTTER AND THE SORCERER'S STONE

Today, I was energized when...   TIME   :

_____

_____

My energy dropped when...

_____

_____

This evening, I am grateful for...

_____

_____

M T W T F S S   DATE   /   /   TIME   :

I feel...   (compassionate)   (dazed)   (fascinated)   (guilty)
_____   (moved)   (offended)   (thankful)   (uneasy)

This morning, I am grateful for...

_____

_____

I will make today enjoyable and interesting by...

_____

_____

I will help others by...

_____

_____

**If you go out and make some good things happen, you will
fill the world with hope, you will fill yourself with hope.**

BARACK OBAMA (B. 1961) 44TH PRESIDENT OF THE UNITED STATES

Today, I was energized when...   TIME   :

_____

_____

My energy dropped when...

_____

_____

This evening, I am grateful for...

_____

_____

I feel... (confident) (defensive) (fearless) (hateful)

_____ (open) (outraged) (thrilled) (unhappy)

This morning, I am grateful for...

_____

_____

I will make today enjoyable and interesting by...

_____

_____

I will help others by...

_____

_____

> When you get into a tight place and everything goes against you, till it seems as though you could not hang on a minute longer, never give up then, for that is just the place and time that the tide will turn.
>
> HARRIET BEECHER STOWE (1811–1896) AUTHOR OF UNCLE TOM'S CABIN

Today, I was energized when...   TIME   :

_____

_____

My energy dropped when...

_____

_____

This evening, I am grateful for...

_____

_____

RELEASE WHAT IS NO LONGER SERVING YOU

Go for a hike. Take an empty backpack. Find a mountain or hill. As you walk up, pick up 10 rocks along the way and put them in your pack. Each rock symbolizes something weighing you down, such as worry or shame. At the top of the hill, toss those rocks away. What did your rocks symbolize? How did it feel to let them go?

M   T   W   T   F   S   S   DATE   /   /   TIME   :

I feel...   (connected)   (detached)   (fired up)   (heartbroken)

_____   (open hearted) (overwhelmed) (tranquil)   (uninterested)

This morning, I am grateful for...

_____

_____

I will make today enjoyable and interesting by...

_____

_____

I will help others by...

_____

_____

> And the day came when the risk to remain tight in a
> bud was more painful than the risk it took to blossom.
>
> ANAIS NIN (1903–1977) FRENCH–BORN AMERICAN ESSAYIST AND MEMOIRIST

Today, I was energized when...   TIME   :

_____

_____

My energy dropped when...

_____

_____

This evening, I am grateful for...

_____

_____

M   T   W   T   F   S   S   DATE   /   /   TIME   :

I feel...   (content)   (disappointed)   (friendly)   (heavy hearted)

_____   (optimistic)   (panicked)   (trusting)   (upset)

This morning, I am grateful for...

_____

_____

I will make today enjoyable and interesting by...

_____

_____

I will help others by...

_____

_____

Courage is not a lack of fear. Courage is dealing with your fear. Nobody would
ever describe someone as courageous who didn't confront their own fear.

KEN ROBINSON (B. 1950) TED SPEAKER AND AUTHOR OF THE ELEMENT

Today, I was energized when...   TIME   :

_____

_____

My energy dropped when...

_____

_____

This evening, I am grateful for...

_____

_____

M   T   W   T   F   S   S   DATE   /   /   TIME   :

I feel...   (courageous)   (disheartened)   (fulfilled)   (helpless)

_____   (overjoyed)   (perplexed)   (unafraid)   (vengeful)

This morning, I am grateful for...

_____

_____

I will make today enjoyable and interesting by...

_____

_____

I will help others by...

_____

_____

You cannot fix what you will not face.

JAMES BALDWIN (1924–1987) AMERICAN NOVELIST, POET, AND SOCIAL CRITIC

Today, I was energized when...   TIME   :

_____

_____

My energy dropped when...

_____

_____

This evening, I am grateful for...

_____

_____

I feel...   (curious)   (disillusioned)   (giddy)   (hesitant)

_____ (passionate)   (petrified)   (vibrant)   (vulnerable)

This morning, I am grateful for...

_____

_____

I will make today enjoyable and interesting by...

_____

_____

I will help others by...

_____

_____

Never do things others can do and will do, if
there are things others cannot do or will not do.

AMELIA EARHART (1897–?) AVIATION PIONEER WHO DISAPPEARED MYSTERIOUSLY

Today, I was energized when...   TIME   :

_____

_____

My energy dropped when...

_____

_____

This evening, I am grateful for...

_____

_____

M   T   W   T   F   S   S   DATE   /   /   TIME   :

I feel...

(dazzled) (distraught) (glad) (hopeless)

_____ (peaceful) (powerless) (warm) (wary)

This morning, I am grateful for...

_____

_____

I will make today enjoyable and interesting by...

_____

_____

I will help others by...

_____

_____

In true courage there is always...a flame of spirit
in it, a vision of some necessity higher than oneself.

BRENDA UELAND (1891–1985) AUTHOR OF IF YOU WANT TO WRITE

Today, I was energized when...   TIME   :

_____

_____

My energy dropped when...

_____

_____

This evening, I am grateful for...

_____

_____

I feel...   (delighted)   (dreadful)   (good)   (horrified)

_____   (pleasant)   (rattled)   (wonderful)   (worried)

This morning, I am grateful for...

_____

_____

I will make today enjoyable and interesting by...

_____

_____

I will help others by...

_____

_____

**To believe yourself to be brave is to
be brave; it is the only essential thing.**

MARK TWAIN (1835–1910) AUTHOR OF THE ADVENTURES OF HUCKLEBERRY FINN

Today, I was energized when...   TIME   :

_____

_____

My energy dropped when...

_____

_____

This evening, I am grateful for...

_____

_____

M T W T F S S   DATE   /   /   TIME   :

I feel...   (eager)   (edgy)   (grateful)   (hostile)

_____   (pleased) (regretful) (wretched) (zen)

This morning, I am grateful for...

_____

_____

I will make today enjoyable and interesting by...

_____

_____

I will help others by...

_____

_____

**Step out of the history that is holding you back.
Step into the new story you are willing to create.**

OPRAH WINFREY (B. 1954) MEDIA ENTREPRENEUR, TALK SHOW HOST, ACTRESS

Today, I was energized when...   TIME   :

_____

_____

My energy dropped when...

_____

_____

This evening, I am grateful for...

_____

_____

ENERGIZE YOUR PRACTICE

LOOK BACK AT YOUR ENTRIES. WHAT GIVES YOU ENERGY?
WHAT TAKES YOUR ENERGY AWAY?

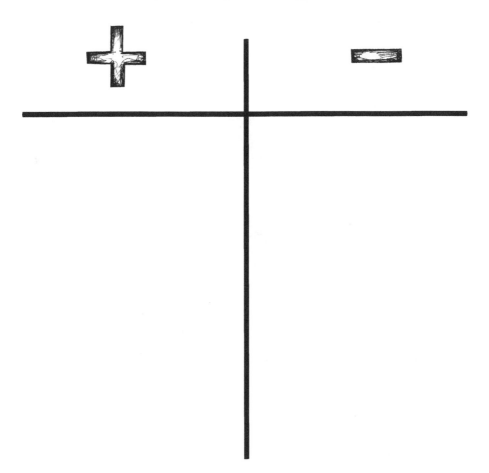

WHAT COULD YOU DO TO DECREASE THE
NEGATIVES AND INCREASE THE POSITIVES?

M   T   W   T   F   S   S   DATE   /   /   TIME   :

I feel...   (absorbed)   (afraid)   (ecstatic)   (embarrassed)
_____ (happy)   (hurt)   (proud)   (remorseful)

This morning, I am grateful for...

_____

_____

I will make today enjoyable and interesting by...

_____

_____

I will help others by...

_____

_____

That's what careless words do. They
make people love you a little less.

ARUNDHATI ROY (B. 1961) INDIAN AUTHOR OF THE GOD OF SMALL THINGS

Today, I was energized when...   TIME   :

_____

_____

My energy dropped when...

_____

_____

This evening, I am grateful for...

_____

_____

M   T   W   T   F   S   S   DATE   /   /   TIME   :

I feel...   (affectionate)   (aggravated)   (elated)   (enraged)

_____ (hopeful)   (impatient)   (quiet)   (removed)

This morning, I am grateful for...

_____

_____

I will make today enjoyable and interesting by...

_____

_____

I will help others by...

_____

_____

> When you are offended at any man's fault, turn to yourself
> and study your own failings. Then you will forget your anger.
>
> EPICTETUS (50–135) GREEK STOIC PHILOSOPHER

Today, I was energized when...   TIME   :

_____

_____

My energy dropped when...

_____

_____

This evening, I am grateful for...

_____

_____

M T W T F S S   DATE   /   /   TIME   :

I feel...   (alert)   (alienated)   (elevated)   (envious)

_____   (huggy)   (insecure)   (radiant)   (repugnant)

This morning, I am grateful for...

_____

_____

I will make today enjoyable and interesting by...

_____

_____

I will help others by...

_____

_____

See the world as your self. Have faith in the way things are.
Love the world as your self; then you can care for all things.

LAO TZU (C. 6TH CENTURY B.C.) CHINESE PHILOSOPHER AND FOUNDER OF TAOISM

Today, I was energized when...   TIME   :

_____

_____

My energy dropped when...

_____

_____

This evening, I am grateful for...

_____

_____

M   T   W   T   F   S   S   DATE   /   /   TIME   :

I feel...   (amazed)   (ambivalent)   (empowered)   (exasperated)

_____   (immersed)   (isolated)   (rapturous)   (repulsed)

This morning, I am grateful for...

_____

_____

I will make today enjoyable and interesting by...

_____

_____

I will help others by...

_____

_____

**A man too busy to take care of his health is like
a mechanic too busy to take care of his tools.**

SPANISH SAYING

Today, I was energized when...   TIME   :

_____

_____

My energy dropped when...

_____

_____

This evening, I am grateful for...

_____

_____

M   T   W   T   F   S   S   DATE   /   /   TIME   :

I feel...   (amused)   (angry)   (enchanted)   (exhausted)

_____ (inspired)   (jealous)   (reassured)   (resentful)

This morning, I am grateful for...

_____

_____

I will make today enjoyable and interesting by...

_____

_____

I will help others by...

_____

_____

When you discover something that nourishes your soul and
brings joy, care enough to make room for it in your life.

JEAN SHINODA BOLEN (B. 1936) AMERICAN PSYCHIATRIST AND JUNGIAN ANALYST

Today, I was energized when...   TIME   :

_____

_____

My energy dropped when...

_____

_____

This evening, I am grateful for...

_____

_____

I feel...   (animated)   (annoyed)   (encouraged)   (fearful)

_____   (interested)   (jittery)   (refreshed)   (reserved)

This morning, I am grateful for...

_____

_____

I will make today enjoyable and interesting by...

_____

_____

I will help others by...

_____

_____

You know that you can't really make much of a difference in things until you change yourself.

ALICE WALKER (B. 1944) NOVELIST AND AUTHOR OF THE COLOR PURPLE

Today, I was energized when...   TIME   :

_____

_____

My energy dropped when...

_____

_____

This evening, I am grateful for...

_____

_____

M T W T F S S   DATE   /   /   TIME   :

I feel...   (appreciative) (apprehensive) (energetic) (fidgety)
_____   (jovial)   (leery)   (rejuvenated) (resigned)

This morning, I am grateful for...

_____

_____

I will make today enjoyable and interesting by...

_____

_____

I will help others by...

_____

_____

When you're in a rut, you have to question
everything except your ability to get out of it.

TWYLA THARP (B. 1941) CHOREOGRAPHER AND AUTHOR OF THE CREATIVE HABIT

Today, I was energized when...   TIME   :

_____

_____

My energy dropped when...

_____

_____

This evening, I am grateful for...

_____

_____

may i be peaceful
may i be happy
may i live with ease

may you be peaceful
may you be happy
may you live with ease

may all beings be peaceful
may all beings be happy
may all beings live with ease

M   T   W   T   F   S   S   DATE   /   /   TIME   :

I feel...   (ardent)   (argumentative)   (energized)   (flustered)

_____   (joyful)   (lethargic)   (relaxed)   (restless)

This morning, I am grateful for...

_____

_____

I will make today enjoyable and interesting by...

_____

_____

I will help others by...

_____

_____

running away from an emotion. is a sure way to carry it with you.

NAYYIRAH WAHEED, INSTAGRAM POET AND AUTHOR OF SALT

Today, I was energized when...   TIME   :

_____

_____

My energy dropped when...

_____

_____

This evening, I am grateful for...

_____

_____

I feel...   aroused   ashamed   engaged   foreboding
_____   jubilant   listless   relieved   revolted

This morning, I am grateful for...

_____

_____

I will make today enjoyable and interesting by...

_____

_____

I will help others by...

_____

_____

> Why do you want to shut out of your life any uneasiness,
> any misery, any depression, since after all you don't know
> what work these conditions are doing inside you?
> RAINER MARIA RILKE (1875–1926) BOHEMIAN–AUSTRIAN POET

Today, I was energized when...   TIME   :

_____

_____

My energy dropped when...

_____

_____

This evening, I am grateful for...

_____

_____

M T W T F S S   DATE   /   /   TIME   :

I feel...   (astonished)   (avoidant)   (engrossed)   (forlorn)
_____   (intrigued)   (livid)   (rested)   (sad)

This morning, I am grateful for...

_____

_____

I will make today enjoyable and interesting by...

_____

_____

I will help others by...

_____

_____

Even a happy life cannot be without a measure of darkness, and the
word happy would lose its meaning if it were not balanced by sadness.

CARL JUNG (1875–1961) SWISS PSYCHIATRIST AND PSYCHOANALYST

Today, I was energized when...   TIME   :

_____

_____

My energy dropped when...

_____

_____

This evening, I am grateful for...

_____

_____

M T W T F S S   DATE   /   /   TIME   :

I feel...   (at ease)   (baffled)   (enthralled)   (fragile)

_____   (invigorated) (loathing)   (safe)   (scared)

This morning, I am grateful for...

_____

_____

I will make today enjoyable and interesting by...

_____

_____

I will help others by...

_____

_____

The strengthening of spiritual practice will help one to overcome
the feelings of inner oppression which lead to exhaustion.

I CHING (C. 1150 B.C.) ANCIENT CHINESE TEXT, KNOWN AS BOOK OF CHANGES

Today, I was energized when...   TIME   :

_____

_____

My energy dropped when...

_____

_____

This evening, I am grateful for...

_____

_____

I feel...

| awed | betrayed | enthusiastic | frazzled |
| involved | lonely | satisfied | tearful |

_____

This morning, I am grateful for...

_____

_____

I will make today enjoyable and interesting by...

_____

_____

I will help others by...

_____

_____

> Now matter how bad a state of mind you may get into, if
> you keep strong and hold out, eventually the floating clouds
> must vanish and the withering winds must cease.
> DŌGEN ZENJI (1200–1253) FOUNDER OF THE SŌTŌ SCHOOL OF ZEN IN JAPAN

Today, I was energized when...   TIME   :

_____

_____

My energy dropped when...

_____

_____

This evening, I am grateful for...

_____

_____

I feel... (blissful) (bored) (entranced) (frightened)

_____ (kind) (lost) (secure) (tense)

This morning, I am grateful for...

_____

_____

I will make today enjoyable and interesting by...

_____

_____

I will help others by...

_____

_____

> If you are depressed you are living in the past. If you are anxious you are
> living in the future. If you are at peace you are living in the present.
>
> LAO TZU (C. 6TH CENTURY B.C.) CHINESE PHILOSOPHER AND FOUNDER OF TAOISM

Today, I was energized when...   TIME   :

_____

_____

My energy dropped when...

_____

_____

This evening, I am grateful for...

_____

_____

M   T   W   T   F   S   S   DATE   /   /   TIME   :

I feel...   (bold)   (burned out)   (equanimous)   (frustrated)

_____   (lighthearted)   (melancholy)   (self-assured)   (terrified)

This morning, I am grateful for...

_____

_____

I will make today enjoyable and interesting by...

_____

_____

I will help others by...

_____

_____

**I got the blues thinking of the future,
so I left off and made some marmalade.**

D. H. LAWRENCE (1885–1930) ENGLISH NOVELIST, POET, AND PAINTER

Today, I was energized when...   TIME   :

_____

_____

My energy dropped when...

_____

_____

This evening, I am grateful for...

_____

_____

EXPLORE YOUR EMOTIONS

In person, on social media, by email or text, ask your friends to "Name three emotions I make you feel." Put their answers in the good, better, best diagram.

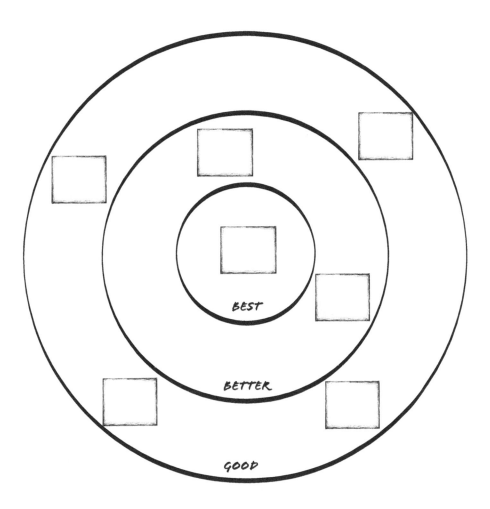

BEST

BETTER

GOOD

WHAT DID YOU DISCOVER?

M T W T F S S   DATE   /   /   TIME   :

I feel...

| calm | cautious | excited | furious |
| lively | miserable | serene | tired |

_____

This morning, I am grateful for...

_____

_____

I will make today enjoyable and interesting by...

_____

_____

I will help others by...

_____

_____

Life isn't about finding yourself. Life is about creating yourself.

GEORGE BERNARD SHAW (1856–1950) IRISH PLAYWRIGHT

Today, I was energized when...   TIME   :

_____

_____

My energy dropped when...

_____

_____

This evening, I am grateful for...

_____

_____

M T W T F S S   DATE   /   /   TIME   :

I feel...   (caring)   (concerned)   (exhilarated)   (gloomy)
_____   (lovey-dovey) (mistrustful)   (spellbound)   (torn)

This morning, I am grateful for...

_____

_____

I will make today enjoyable and interesting by...

_____

_____

I will help others by...

_____

_____

Be mindful of intention. Intention is
the seed that creates our future.

JACK KORNFIELD (B. 1945) MEDITATION TEACHER, AUTHOR OF THE WISE HEART

Today, I was energized when...   TIME   :

_____

_____

My energy dropped when...

_____

_____

This evening, I am grateful for...

_____

_____

M   T   W   T   F   S   S   DATE   /   /   TIME   :

I feel...   (centered)   (confused)   (expansive)   (grieved)

_____   (loving)   (nervous)   (steady)   (troubled)

This morning, I am grateful for...

_____

_____

I will make today enjoyable and interesting by...

_____

_____

I will help others by...

_____

_____

The consequences of today are determined by the actions of the past. To change your future, alter your decisions today.

S. N. GOENKA (1924–2013) BURMESE–INDIAN TEACHER OF VIPASSANÁ MEDITATION

Today, I was energized when...   TIME   :

_____

_____

My energy dropped when...

_____

_____

This evening, I am grateful for...

_____

_____

I feel...   (clear headed) (contemptuous) (expectant) (grumpy)

_____   (mellow) (nostalgic) (still) (turbulent)

This morning, I am grateful for...

_____

_____

I will make today enjoyable and interesting by...

_____

_____

I will help others by...

_____

_____

**Good judgment is the result of experience
and experience the result of bad judgment.**

MARK TWAIN (1835–1910) AUTHOR OF THE ADVENTURES OF HUCKLEBERRY FINN

Today, I was energized when...   TIME   :

_____

_____

My energy dropped when...

_____

_____

This evening, I am grateful for...

_____

_____

I feel...
| comfortable | cranky | exuberant | guarded |
| motivated | numb | tender | uncomfortable |

_____

This morning, I am grateful for...

_____

_____

I will make today enjoyable and interesting by...

_____

_____

I will help others by...

_____

_____

> To make no mistake is not in the power of man; but from their error
> and mistakes the wise and good learn wisdom for the future.
>
> PLUTARCH (C. 45–120) GREEK BIOGRAPHER AND ESSAYIST

Today, I was energized when...   TIME :

_____

_____

My energy dropped when...

_____

_____

This evening, I am grateful for...

_____

_____

I feel...

| compassionate | dazed | fascinated | guilty |
| moved | offended | thankful | uneasy |

_____

This morning, I am grateful for...

_____

_____

I will make today enjoyable and interesting by...

_____

_____

I will help others by...

_____

_____

> Men are only free when they're doing what the deepest self likes.
> And there is getting down to the deepest self! It takes some diving.
>
> D. H. LAWRENCE (1885–1930) ENGLISH NOVELIST, POET, AND PAINTER

Today, I was energized when...   TIME   :

_____

_____

My energy dropped when...

_____

_____

This evening, I am grateful for...

_____

_____

M   T   W   T   F   S   S   DATE   /   /   TIME   :

I feel...   (confident)   (defensive)   (fearless)   (hateful)
_____   (open   )   (outraged)   (thrilled)   (unhappy)

This morning, I am grateful for...

_____

_____

I will make today enjoyable and interesting by...

_____

_____

I will help others by...

_____

_____

What is your deepest intention right now?

TARA BRACH (B. 1953) MEDITATION TEACHER, AUTHOR OF RADICAL ACCEPTANCE

Today, I was energized when...   TIME   :

_____

_____

My energy dropped when...

_____

_____

This evening, I am grateful for...

_____

_____

SET YOUR INTENTIONS

Collect your favorite quotes from the journal

M   T   W   T   F   S   S   DATE   /   /   TIME   :

I feel...   (connected)   (detached)   (fired up)   (heartbroken)

_____   (open hearted) (overwhelmed) (tranquil)   (uninterested)

This morning, I am grateful for...

_____

_____

I will make today enjoyable and interesting by...

_____

_____

I will help others by...

_____

_____

Plunge boldly into the thick of life.

JOHANN WOLFGANG VON GOETHE (1749–1832) GERMAN WRITER AND STATESMAN

Today, I was energized when...   TIME   :

_____

_____

My energy dropped when...

_____

_____

This evening, I am grateful for...

_____

_____

DATE   /   /   TIME   :

I feel...

content <button>disappointed</button> <button>friendly</button> <button>heavy hearted</button>

_____

optimistic <button>panicked</button> <button>trusting</button> <button>upset</button>

This morning, I am grateful for...

_____

_____

I will make today enjoyable and interesting by...

_____

_____

I will help others by...

_____

_____

What hunger is in relation to food, zest is in relation to life.

BERTRAND RUSSELL (1872–1970) PHILOSOPHER AND NOBEL PRIZE WINNER

Today, I was energized when...   TIME   :

_____

_____

My energy dropped when...

_____

_____

This evening, I am grateful for...

_____

_____

M   T   W   T   F   S   S   DATE   /   /   TIME   :

I feel...
(courageous) (disheartened) (fulfilled) (helpless)
_____
(overjoyed) (perplexed) (unafraid) (vengeful)

This morning, I am grateful for...

_____

_____

I will make today enjoyable and interesting by...

_____

_____

I will help others by...

_____

_____

He who possesses the source of enthusiasm will achieve great things. Doubt not. You will gather friends around you as a hair clasp gathers the hair.

I CHING (C. 1150 B.C.) ANCIENT CHINESE TEXT, KNOWN AS BOOK OF CHANGES

Today, I was energized when...   TIME   :

_____

_____

My energy dropped when...

_____

_____

This evening, I am grateful for...

_____

_____

I feel...   (curious) (disillusioned) (giddy) (hesitant)

_____   (passionate) (petrified) (vibrant) (vulnerable)

This morning, I am grateful for...

_____

_____

I will make today enjoyable and interesting by...

_____

_____

I will help others by...

_____

_____

> From now on I will make burning my aim, for
> I am like a candle: burning only makes me brighter.
>
> RUMI (1207–1273) PERSIAN POET, SCHOLAR, THEOLOGIAN, AND SUFI MYSTIC

Today, I was energized when...   TIME   :

_____

_____

My energy dropped when...

_____

_____

This evening, I am grateful for...

_____

_____

I feel... | dazzled | | distraught | | glad | | hopeless |

_____ | peaceful | | powerless | | warm | | wary |

This morning, I am grateful for...

_____

_____

I will make today enjoyable and interesting by...

_____

_____

I will help others by...

_____

_____

The way of life is wonderful; it is by abandonment.

RALPH WALDO EMERSON (1803–1882) AMERICAN PHILOSOPHER AND POET

Today, I was energized when...   TIME   :

_____

_____

My energy dropped when...

_____

_____

This evening, I am grateful for...

_____

_____

M   T   W   T   F   S   S   DATE   /   /   TIME   :

I feel...   (delighted)   (dreadful)   (good)   (horrified)
_____   (pleasant)   (rattled)   (wonderful)   (worried)

This morning, I am grateful for...

_____

_____

I will make today enjoyable and interesting by...

_____

_____

I will help others by...

_____

_____

The life that is worth living, and the only life that is worth living, is
the life of effort, the life of effort to attain what is worth striving for.

THEODORE ROOSEVELT (1858–1919) 26TH PRESIDENT OF THE UNITED STATES

Today, I was energized when...   TIME   :

_____

_____

My energy dropped when...

_____

_____

This evening, I am grateful for...

_____

_____

M   T   W   T   F   S   S   DATE   /   /   TIME   :

I feel...   (eager)   (edgy)   (grateful)   (hostile)

_____   (pleased)   (regretful)   (wretched)   (zen)

This morning, I am grateful for...

_____

_____

I will make today enjoyable and interesting by...

_____

_____

I will help others by...

_____

_____

**What is required is sight and insight —
then you might add one more: excite.**

ROBERT FROST (1874–1963) FOUR-TIME WINNER OF THE PULITZER PRIZE IN POETRY

Today, I was energized when...   TIME   :

_____

_____

My energy dropped when...

_____

_____

This evening, I am grateful for...

_____

_____

THE CIRCLE OF LIFE

WHAT ARE FIVE THINGS YOU ABSOLUTELY WANT IN YOUR LIFE?
WRITE THOSE INSIDE THE CIRCLE. WHAT ARE FIVE THINGS YOU DO
NOT WANT IN YOUR LIFE? WRITE THOSE OUTSIDE THE CIRCLE.

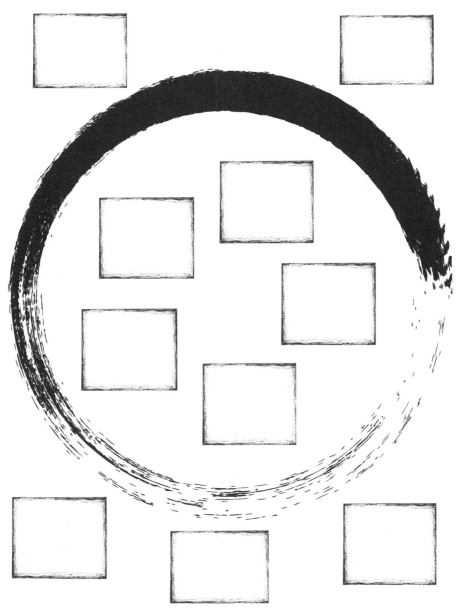

I feel...
_____

(absorbed)   (afraid)   (ecstatic)   (embarrassed)
(happy)   (hurt)   (proud)   (remorseful)

This morning, I am grateful for...

_____

_____

I will make today enjoyable and interesting by...

_____

_____

I will help others by...

_____

_____

My first commandment is to "Be Gretchen" – yet it's very hard to
know myself. I get so distracted by the way I wish I were, or
the way I assume I am, that I lose sight of what's actually true.
GRETCHEN RUBIN (B. 1965) AUTHOR OF THE HAPPINESS PROJECT

Today, I was energized when...   TIME   :

_____

_____

My energy dropped when...

_____

_____

This evening, I am grateful for...

_____

_____

I feel...
_____

| affectionate | aggravated | elated | enraged |
| hopeful | impatient | quiet | removed |

This morning, I am grateful for...

_____

_____

I will make today enjoyable and interesting by...

_____

_____

I will help others by...

_____

_____

**There are three things extremely hard:
steel, a diamond, and to know one's self.**

BENJAMIN FRANKLIN (1706–1790) AUTHOR OF POOR RICHARD'S ALMANACK

Today, I was energized when...   TIME   :

_____

_____

My energy dropped when...

_____

_____

This evening, I am grateful for...

_____

_____

I feel...

alert	alienated	elevated	envious
huggy	insecure	radiant	repugnant

_____

This morning, I am grateful for...

_____

_____

I will make today enjoyable and interesting by...

_____

_____

I will help others by...

_____

_____

The soul must always stand ajar,
ready to welcome the ecstatic experience.

EMILY DICKINSON (1830–1886) AMERICAN POET

Today, I was energized when...   TIME   :

_____

_____

My energy dropped when...

_____

_____

This evening, I am grateful for...

_____

_____

M   T   W   T   F   S   S   DATE   /   /   TIME   :

I feel...

(amazed) (ambivalent) (empowered) (exasperated)

_____ (immersed) (isolated) (rapturous) (repulsed)

This morning, I am grateful for...

_____

_____

I will make today enjoyable and interesting by...

_____

_____

I will help others by...

_____

_____

The Master observes the world but trusts her inner vision.
She allows things to come and go. Her heart is open as the sky.

LAO TZU (C. 6TH CENTURY B.C.) CHINESE PHILOSOPHER AND FOUNDER OF TAOISM

Today, I was energized when...   TIME   :

_____

_____

My energy dropped when...

_____

_____

This evening, I am grateful for...

_____

_____

I feel...

_____

(amused)   (angry)   (enchanted)   (exhausted)
(inspired)   (jealous)   (reassured)   (resentful)

This morning, I am grateful for...

_____

_____

I will make today enjoyable and interesting by...

_____

_____

I will help others by...

_____

_____

We have all a better guide in ourselves, if we
would attend to it, than any other person can be.

JANE AUSTEN (1775–1817) NOVELIST, AUTHOR OF PRIDE AND PREJUDICE

Today, I was energized when...   TIME   :

_____

_____

My energy dropped when...

_____

_____

This evening, I am grateful for...

_____

_____

M   T   W   T   F   S   S   DATE   /   /   TIME   :

I feel...   (animated)   (annoyed)   (encouraged)   (fearful)

_____   (interested)   (jittery)   (refreshed)   (reserved)

This morning, I am grateful for...

_____

_____

I will make today enjoyable and interesting by...

_____

_____

I will help others by...

_____

_____

I wish I could show you when you are lonely or in
darkness the astonishing light of your own being.

HAFIZ (1315–1390) PERSIAN POET

Today, I was energized when...   TIME   :

_____

_____

My energy dropped when...

_____

_____

This evening, I am grateful for...

_____

_____

M   T   W   T   F   S   S   DATE   /   /   TIME   :

I feel...   (appreciative)   (apprehensive)   (energetic)   (fidgety)

_____   (jovial)   (leery)   (rejuvenated) (resigned)

This morning, I am grateful for...

_____

_____

I will make today enjoyable and interesting by...

_____

_____

I will help others by...

_____

_____

You yourself, as much as anybody in the
entire universe, deserve your love and affection.

BUDDHA (C. 6TH CENTURY B.C.) INDIAN ASCETIC AND SAGE

Today, I was energized when...   TIME   :

_____

_____

My energy dropped when...

_____

_____

This evening, I am grateful for...

_____

_____

CONGRATULATIONS!

YOU'VE DONE IT! YOU'VE FINISHED!

As Chinese philosopher Lao Tzu said, "The journey of a thousand miles begins with one step." Spending three months with this journal is a small but significant step on the life-long journey of mindful living.

By cultivating mindfulness of your emotions, intentions, and energy you have been watching after yourself, and, in turn, watching after others.

Savor this moment. How does it feel?

Now it's time to integrate your experience. Turn the page and write about what you've learned about yourself.

WRITE TO DISCOVER

WHAT HAVE YOU LEARNED ABOUT YOURSELF?

ABOUT THE AUTHOR

Across 5 continents, 39 countries, and 48 U.S. states, by ship, train, plane, bus, rickshaw, bicycle, camel, and motorcycle, Justin R. Adams has sought out experiences that foster insight. His interest in Buddhism and mindfulness began when he lived in South Korea, continued in India, and culminated in Ann Arbor.

A curious learner and creative thinker, and compelling storyteller, he helps people see the big picture in a way they never have before. By asking powerful questions and making unexpected connections, he helps others advance their thinking and approach so they can continue to improve and innovate.

Inspired by the Vipassanā meditation retreats he attends, he set out to make *The Mindful Life Journal* an immersive, transformational experience. This is his first book.

ACKNOWLEDGEMENTS

THIS JOURNAL IS THE RESULT of months of work by dozens of people.

First off, I would like to acknowledge the members of my "advance team." These beta journalers volunteered to test early prototypes of the journal and provide feedback. This book would not be as good as it is without their help. In alphabetical order by first name, they are:

Angela Flood, Beni Chhun, Brian Raisbeck, Catie Anderson, Chris Mueller, Chris White, Cyndy Cleveland, Elizabeth Stamberger, Emily Adama, Emily Howard, Janette Reynolds, Jason Howell, Jeanette Wardynski, Jennifer Yim, Jenny Casler, Jim Kleiber, John Lankeu, John Schwab, Justin House, Justin Manning, Kara Davidson, Karl Rosaen, Laura Palombi, Lee Alexander, Leonore Adams, Lindsay Boyce, Mary Ellen Adams, Max Smouha, Nathan Meffert, Nehemiah Harmsen, Nicole Bishop, Patricia Griffin, Ryan Chylinski, Sam Smouha, Sarah Monje, Seth Kopald, Stephanie Judd, Susan Bernstein, Tal Avrahami, Tamasin Ford, Terrence Campagna, and Virginia Boyce.

Each of you provided a piece of feedback, a suggestion, a resource, or an ear when I need one that helped bring this project to fruition. Thank you so much for joining me on this journey.

Thanks also to Jane Dutton and Chen Zhang for pointing me in the direction of the science of human energy — Google Scholar has indeed become a good friend; to Dr. James Bramson for having me do the rock exercise a few years ago; to Alex Linkow, Amrita V.K. Vatsal, Sean Killian, and Omar Wasow for providing stabilizing perspectives when I needed them the most; to Kathryn Kempton Amaral for turning me onto the poetry of Nayyirah Waheed; and to Candy Chang for Instagramming about emotional granularity. Before I die I want to write a novel. You heard it here first.

This journal would not have been possible without the support of Haju Sunim, Maum, and the other residents at the Zen Buddhist Temple in Ann Arbor. It also benefited from the financial support of friends and family. Special thanks to Chris Mueller, Virginia Boyce, and my parents, Richard and Mary Ellen Adams.

I've had many virtual mentors along the way to publication. Joanna Penn's podcast served as the spine of my learning journey. Through her, I discovered and benefited from the indie publishing insights of Data Guy, Joel Friedlander, Tim Grahl, Shawn Coyne, Derek

Murphy, Chris Fox, Nick Stephenson, Mark Dawson, the Two Marks of the Bestseller Experiment, Mark Coker, and more.

Thanks to Jerome Ware for turning me on to the potential of print-on-demand publishing. I am blown away by the infrastructure that has emerged in the last ten years to make it possible to publish globally from a five year old laptop.

Thanks to Vikncharlie for working with me to create a cover I love, and to annabazyl for adding a little whimsy to the journal through her delightful illustrations.

Finally, I would like to offer my sincere thanks to Jeff and Staney DeGraff, as well as Sarah Hussong, for allowing me to camp out in the back corner of the Innovatrium for the past year. Your continued generosity means a lot to me. Plus, I can hardly think without a wall-sized whiteboard to write on anymore!

With a deep bow to one and all,
Justin

ABOUT BETTER LIFE JOURNALS

Based in leafy, intellectual Ann Arbor, Michigan, we use the best of ancient Eastern wisdom and modern Western science to create journals that help people live better lives. *The Mindful Life Journal* is our first title. We have many more in the works. Learn more at our website, www.betterlifejournals.com.

If *The Mindful Life Journal* has helped you, please consider helping others create better, more meaningful lives for themselves by:

- Telling a friend, colleague, or loved one about this journal
- Giving them a copy of the journal as a gift
- Writing an honest review on Amazon or Goodreads
- Forming a mindfulness-based journaling Meetup group
- Continuing to integrate mindfulness into your daily life

Thank you for creating a more mindful world.

pause
breathe
listen